OUT OF THIS WORLD

Meet NASA Inventor Masahiro Ono and His Team's

Asteroid- Harpooning Hitcher

WORLD BOOK

www.worldbook.com

World Book, Inc.
180 North LaSalle Street
Suite 900
Chicago, Illinois 60601
USA

For information about other World Book publications, visit our website at www.worldbook.com or call 1-800-WORLDBK (967-5325).

For information about sales to schools and libraries, call 1-800-975-3250 (United States), or 1-800-837-5365 (Canada).

Library of Congress Cataloging-in-Publication Data for this volume has been applied for.

Out of This World
978-0-7166-6155-9 (set, hc.)

Asteroid-Harpooning Hitcher
ISBN: 978-0-7166-6161-0 (hc.)

Also available as:
ISBN: 978-0-7166-6170-2 (e-book)

Printed in China by Shenzhen Donnelley Printing Co., Ltd., Guangdong Province
1st printing June 2017

Staff

Writer: Jeff De La Rosa

Executive Committee

President
Jim O'Rourke

Vice President and
Editor in Chief
Paul A. Kobasa

Vice President, Finance
Donald D. Keller

Vice President, Marketing
Jean Lin

Vice President, International Sales
Maksim Rutenberg

Director, Human Resources
Bev Ecker

Editorial

Director, Print Content
Development
Tom Evans

Editor, Print Content Development
Kendra Muntz

Managing Editor, Science
Jeff De La Rosa

Editor, Science
William D. Adams

Librarian
S. Thomas Richardson

Manager, Contracts & Compliance
(Rights & Permissions)
Loranne K. Shields

Manager, Indexing Services
David Pofelski

Administrative Assistant, Digital
and Print Content Development
Ethel Matthews

Digital

Director, Digital Content
Development
Emily Kline

Director, Digital Product
Development
Erika Meller

Manager, Digital Products
Jonathan Wills

Graphics and Design

Senior Art Director
Tom Evans

Senior Visual Communications
Designer
Melanie Bender

Media Researcher
Rosalia Bledsoe

Manufacturing/ Production

Manufacturing Manager
Anne Fritzinger

Proofreader
Nathalie Strassheim

Contents

Glossary There is a glossary of terms on page 45. Terms defined in the glossary are in boldface type that **looks like this** on their first appearance on any spread (two facing pages).

Pronunciations (how to say words) are given in parentheses the first time some difficult words appear in the book. They look like this: pronunciation (pruh NUHN see AY shuhn).

Introduction

Getting a spacecraft to a distant planet, moon, or other object in space may seem like a difficult task. But stopping the craft when it gets to the object can be an even greater challenge. In a speeding automobile, you can simply hit the brakes. The tires grip the road, bringing the vehicle to a halt. But in space, there is no road and nothing else to grip.

Scientists know that it's easier to slow a spacecraft down when it is approaching a large object. Imagine a robotic space **probe** sent to study the planet Jupiter. To make the long journey, the probe must travel at extremely high speeds. But once the probe reaches Jupiter, the planet's tremendous **gravitational pull** helps to reel the craft in. It only takes a little timely firing of the spacecraft's engine to allow the craft to enter **orbit.** The probe can then circle Jupiter for months or even years, observing the planet and conducting experiments.

Now imagine a probe sent to a much smaller object—an **asteroid.** To get there, the probe must still travel at high speeds. But the asteroid has a much smaller **mass** than Jupiter. So, the asteroid has a much weaker gravitational pull. A weak gravitational pull makes it much more difficult for the probe to change direction and follow the asteroid through space. The probe can conduct a **fly-by** visit, snapping a few photos as it whizzes past. But without an extremely long burn of its engine, it may be unable to avoid rapidly flying off into space.

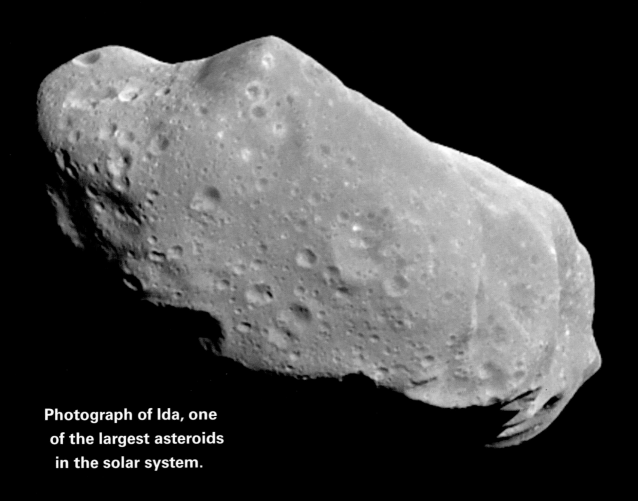

Photograph of Ida, one of the largest asteroids in the solar system.

Engineer Masahiro Ono wants to send a probe to an asteroid or similar small body. But rather than just breezing by, he would like the probe to stay and gather information for research. Ono's probe would not rely on the asteroid's gravitational pull to go into orbit. Instead, as it flies by its target, the craft would shoot the asteroid with a harpoon attached to a long **tether.** By releasing more of the tether, the probe could gradually slow itself in relation to the target. Then the probe could reel in the tether, pulling itself in for a landing.

It all sounds pretty simple, until you take into account the tremendous speeds and forces involved. The harpoon and tether would have to be made from the toughest materials available. Also, new technologies would be required to slow the craft without destroying it.

The challenges are great, but so are the possible rewards. Our **solar system** includes thousands of asteroids, comets, and other small bodies. These are the "crumbs" left over from the formation of the sun, the planets, and their moons. By hooking up to these crumbs for extended observations, Ono's asteroid-harpooning hitcher might help us answer important questions about the solar system's origins.

Harpoons were widely used by the whaling industry in the 1800's.

The NASA Innovative Advanced Concepts program. The titles in the *Out of This World* series feature projects that have won grant money from a group formed by the United States National Aeronautics and Space Administration, or NASA. The NASA Innovative Advanced Concepts program (NIAC) provides funding to teams working to develop bold new advances in space technology. You can visit NIAC's website at www.nasa.gov/niac.

Meet Masahiro Ono.

" Hello, I am Masahiro Ono, (Hiro for short), an engineer at NASA's Jet Propulsion Laboratory in Pasadena, California. As a young man, I backpacked around the world, hitching my way from one exotic destination to the next. Now I am working to build a probe that can hitch itself to an asteroid. "

The leftovers

Scientists think that our **solar system** formed billions of years ago. It all started with a giant cloud of gas and dust in space. At some point in time, part of the cloud began to *contract* (pull together) under the influence of gravity. As the cloud contracted, it spun faster and faster.

Much of the cloud's material was drawn together, forming what would become the sun. The rest of the cloud continued to swirl around the sun. As the cloud swirled, particles collided and stuck together, forming chunks called **planetesimals.** Many planetesimals, in turn, collided and stuck together, forming bigger and bigger masses. This is how the planets and moons of our solar system were formed.

But not all of the particles were absorbed by the planets and moons. Some chunks failed to reach a large size. Others collided and broke apart into smaller pieces. These pieces are the "leftovers" of planetary formation.

One major class of leftovers is the **asteroids.** There may be millions of asteroids in our solar system. Most asteroids circle the sun between the orbits of the planets Mars and Jupiter. This region is known as the Main Belt.

Another region where many leftovers are found is the **Kuiper belt.** The Kuiper (*KY pur*) belt lies in the outer solar system, extending beyond the orbit of the planet Neptune. The small bodies found there are called **Kuiper belt objects** (KBO's). They are similar to asteroids in some ways, but KBO's are icy, rather than rocky. The dwarf planet Pluto is the Kuiper belt's most famous resident.

A few asteroids and KBO's are large enough to be considered dwarf planets. But most of these objects are small and widely separated.

Why study the leftovers?

Scientists are fascinated by such leftovers as **asteroids** and **Kuiper belt objects** (KBO's) in part because they preserve evidence from the early **solar system.**

To understand why, think of the **planetesimals** that collided to form Earth. As these chunks smashed together, their collisions generated great heat and melted much of the growing planet. Due to the force of gravity, the melted rock separated to form layers. The heavier materials sank to Earth's center, and the lighter rocks rose to the surface and eventually cooled. Over billions of years, the surface rocks have continued to be changed by volcanic eruptions and other geological activity. They have been weathered, broken down, and remade.

Earth's rocks have changed so much over time that very little evidence has been preserved from the early solar system. Asteroids and KBO's, on the other hand, have spent the last 5 billion years in the cold, airless freezer of space. There, they have remained mostly unchanged, waiting to be analyzed by space missions.

The New Horizons probe will fly past a small Kuiper belt object in 2019.

Inventor feature:
The traveler

Hiro Ono has always been interested in exploration. Long before he set his sights on the **asteroids,** he traveled the world as an Earth-bound voyager.

" I was a backpacker. I am still a backpacker in my mind. I like to go to places that I have not seen before. **"** —Hiro

Ono has visited more than 30 countries, including India and China. He has traveled on different continents, including Africa and South America.

" Part of the joy of traveling is to find something new and to meet a kind of person that you would never meet in your daily life. Each country has its own color and its own flavor. **"** —Hiro

Ono also enjoys the challenge of visiting unfamiliar parts of the world. He likes to visit places that are difficult to reach.

❚❚ In the United States and many other parts of the world, you can just search the Internet and develop a precise itinerary. Just follow the itinerary, and you arrive at the scheduled time. I like going places where you have to ask the local people [what to do and how to get around]. You may not know the language, but it is amazing how much you can communicate with just a few basic words and the pointing of fingers. ❚❚
—Hiro

Such rough travel is not without its troubles. Ono once had all of his money stolen and, after injuring his foot in Gambia, received stitches without the benefit of anesthetic (pain-numbing) medication.

Hiro poses with the children he met in the Central American country of Nicaragua while on one of his backpacking adventures.

❚❚ That was a tough experience but a good one. Travel shares the same spirit as space exploration. You explore the unknown, and you face troubles. You overcome the troubles. I love it! ❚❚ —Hiro

Visiting the asteroids

Astronomers discovered the first **asteroids** by looking through telescopes in the early 1800's. But the first close-up look at an asteroid did not come until the 1990's.

On its way to Jupiter, the United States **probe** Galileo flew by the asteroids Gaspra in 1991 and Ida in 1993. Galileo shot past Ida at a speed of about 7.7 miles (12.4 kilometers) per second.

❝ At that speed, the craft would take about a minute to travel from San Francisco to Los Angeles, California, a distance of some 380 miles [610 kilometers]. ❞ —Hiro

The **fly-by** encounter only allowed enough time for Galileo to measure the asteroid's **mass** and snap a few pictures. The images revealed that Ida had a tiny satellite, later named Dactyl.

❝ Imagine visiting a city for the first time, and you are on an express train that does not stop there. The express train boldly passes the city at high speed as you observe from the train window. How much can you know about the city? To know better, you want to stay and spend the night, exploring the city. But as it turns out, that is more expensive than you thought. ❞ —Hiro

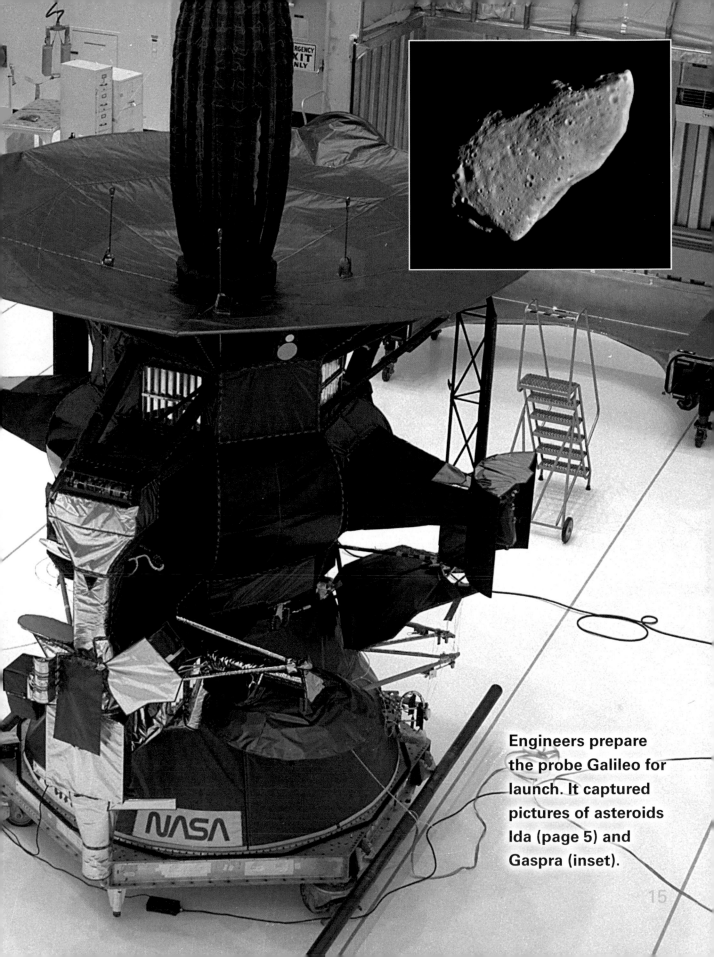

Engineers prepare the probe Galileo for launch. It captured pictures of asteroids Ida (page 5) and Gaspra (inset).

Stopping in

To stop in for a longer visit, a space **probe** must go into **orbit** around its target. A probe in orbit has been captured by its target's **gravitational pull.** This pull draws the craft into a looping path around the target. In orbit, the probe can circle the target over and over, conducting extended observations. From orbit, a craft can also attempt to land on the target.

Whether a probe can enter orbit depends in part on relative velocity. Relative velocity is the difference in speed between two objects: in this case, between the space probe and its target. Relative velocity can be thought of as the speed at which the probe approaches the target.

Space exploration generally involves traveling huge distances. The Galileo probe, for example, had to travel millions of miles or kilometers on its journey to Jupiter. A spacecraft must move very quickly to cover such vast distances in a reasonable time. Remember, for example, that Galileo passed the **asteroid** Ida at a relative velocity of about 7.7 miles (12.4 kilometers) per second. Because spacecraft travel so fast, they must generally slow down to be drawn into orbit.

Just how much a probe has to slow down depends on the strength of its target's gravitational pull. Gravitational pull increases with an object's **mass.** A massive planet such as Jupiter has a powerful gravitational pull. This fact makes it much easier for a fast-moving probe to enter orbit around Jupiter.

An **asteroid** has a much smaller gravitational pull. As a result, a probe has to slow down much more dramatically to enter orbit around it.

❚❚ Going into orbit around an asteroid requires many times as much braking as entering orbit around a planet. In a train, you can just apply the brake and stop. In space, to apply the brake, you need to fire a rocket engine. ❚❚ —Hiro

Rockets require fuel, which is heavy and therefore expensive to launch. The massive amounts of fuel required to "stop" at an asteroid (which is actually speeding around the sun) could make visiting an asteroid difficult and expensive.

The spacecraft Rosetta needed strong rockets to go into orbit around Comet 67P/Churyumov-Gerasimenko, pictured here.

Hitching an asteroid

Perhaps, thought Hiro Ono, a space **probe** might not have to rely on gravity to stop. Ono was listening to a news broadcast about a craft sent to **orbit** another small body, a comet. The broadcast described the difficult and lengthy maneuvers the probe undertook to decrease its relative velocity.

" I was thinking, 'Why is it so difficult to stop? You are passing by the comet. Just throw a rope and catch it!' **"** —Hiro

That thought sparked an idea that could change how people explore outer space. Ono began to envision a craft that would use a harpoon and **tether** to snag the comet as it went by. He called his craft the *Comet Hitchhiker*.

" It turned out, after study, that the best use of the technology would be to orbit and land on asteroids, rather than comets. So we kind of repurposed a little bit. **"** —Hiro

Ono realized that building such an asteroid-hitching craft would involve several major challenges. The biggest challenge would be building a tether strong enough to withstand the incredible force of a hitch at a relative velocity of 6 miles (10 kilometers) per second.

Velocity— It's all relative!

Why do we talk about relative velocity, instead of just "velocity"? In truth, all measurements of velocity are relative, even if we might not think of them that that way. On Earth, we're concerned with how fast an object is moving compared to Earth's surface. For instance, a speed limit sign might restrict cars to traveling at a certain speed. It's understood that the sign is limiting a vehicle's speed relative to Earth's surface, rather than another moving vehicle, the sun, or the moon.

While this arrangement makes sense on Earth's surface, spacecraft exploring the solar system don't always have such a handy reference point. Therefore, scientists might define a craft's relative velocity in terms of the sun or the object it is traveling toward or orbiting, rather than its speed in relation to Earth.

Inventor feature:
Growing up

Hiro Ono grew up in Tokyo, Japan. From an early age, he can remember being interested in science and technology.

❝ In Japan, we have a magazine called *Newton*, somewhat like *National Geographic* in the United States. It covers interesting science stories for a popular audience. **❞** —Hiro

Ono has happy memories of reading the magazine and of watching educational programming on *Newton's* television network. Both Ono and his father, an optical engineer, would enjoy *Newton*, discussing what they had learned. (An optical engineer studies and develops uses of such things as lenses, microscopes, and telescopes.)

❝ The single person who influenced me the most is my father. My father was a great teacher. He never worked as a teacher, but whenever I would ask 'why?,' he was good at explaining things in an intuitive way. **❞** —Hiro

Ono has vivid memories of the space **probe** Voyager 2's 1989 **fly-by** of the planet Neptune.

❝ How can a person not be inspired by that? Voyager had traveled to such a distant place. Here is the *analogy* [comparison] my father used to explain it to me: If Earth were only the size of a marble, Neptune would still be more than 3 miles [5 kilometers] away. Three miles is a great distance for a child! It was farther than my school or any of my friends' homes. That kind of struck me—that humans could send this tiny spacecraft precisely to that far location. **❞** —Hiro

A television crew prepares for live coverage of Voyager 2's Neptune fly-by.

Big idea:
Tethers

A **tether** is basically a long rope connecting two objects. The idea may sound pretty simple, but tethers have a surprising number of potential uses in space exploration. Tethers can be used to link spacewalking astronauts to their craft and to connect two craft together. They could also be used to tow satellites into and out of various **orbits.**

" The obvious challenge in designing a tether is strength. **"**
—Hiro

Many space projects require tethers that are long and strong. The strongest tether yet used in space was made of a high-tech material called Zylon. Zylon is a *synthetic* (manufactured) *polymer*. Polymers are long, chainlike **molecules** made up of smaller chemical units called *monomers*. The chainlike structure and interactions between adjacent chains help to give polymers like Zylon strength and flexibility.

Zylon rope is about 20 times stronger than ordinary rope. Yet Zylon is probably not strong enough to hitch a passing **asteroid.**

" With a Zylon tether, hitching at a **relative velocity** of 0.6 miles [1 kilometer] per second is no problem. Doing 1.2 miles

[2 kilometers] per second is difficult. A hitch at 2.4 miles [4 kilometers] per second is impossible with current technology. For our target velocity of 6 miles [10 kilometers] per second, you need a rope which is at least 20 times stronger than Zylon. **"** —Hiro

To achieve that kind of strength, Ono wants to use one of the strongest fibers known on Earth: carbon nanotubes. A carbon nanotube is a tube-shaped structure of carbon atoms several *nanometers* (billionths of a meter) in diameter.

The space elevator

Tether technology also plays a role in one of the most ambitious exploration technologies ever conceived: the space elevator. The space elevator would consist of a long tether connecting the surface of Earth to a counterweight in orbit. A motorized elevator car could climb the tether, carrying spacecraft into space. The space elevator would reduce the need for rocket launches, making it much easier to get craft into space.

An artist's concept of a space elevator.

Big idea:
Carbon nanotubes

To understand why carbon nanotubes are so tough, think about another material made up of the element carbon—diamond. Diamond is the hardest naturally occurring substance on Earth. The reason has to do with its structure.

Diamond is made up exclusively of carbon atoms. A carbon atom can form up to four chemical bonds with other atoms. In a diamond, each carbon atom is *bound* (connected) to four of its neighbors in a gridlike structure called a lattice. So a diamond is actually just a single giant, interconnected **molecule** of carbon.

A carbon nanotube is also one giant carbon molecule, with each atom bound to several neighbors. But rather than a lattice, the atoms form a long, narrow tube. This arrangement enables the molecule to be flexible, while retaining some of the toughness of diamond.

To reach the necessary length and strength, scientists will have to develop new ways to weave individual nanotube fibers into yarns and ropes.

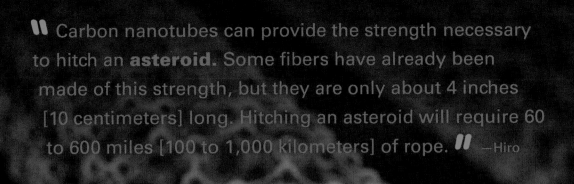

" Carbon nanotubes can provide the strength necessary to hitch an **asteroid.** Some fibers have already been made of this strength, but they are only about 4 inches [10 centimeters] long. Hitching an asteroid will require 60 to 600 miles [100 to 1,000 kilometers] of rope. **"** —Hiro

Carbon nanotubes,
depicted here,
are flexible yet
extremely strong.

Inventor feature:
Crossing the ocean to reach the stars

In 2005, Hiro Ono came to the United States from Japan to study at the Massachusetts Institute of Technology (MIT), a university in the town of Cambridge outside the city of Boston, known worldwide for its science and technology programs. An accomplished student, Ono arrived at MIT confident in his abilities. But he struggled with the language barrier, leading to feelings of *isolation* (loneliness and separateness) both inside and outside the classroom.

❝ My first semester, I took a class on satellite engineering, in which students worked in teams to design a spacecraft. Although my English was well above average for a Japanese student, I was miserable among American students. My ideas, spoken in poor English, could hardly be communicated to the team. Impatient team members often interrupted my slowly spoken and poorly worded remarks. ❞

—Hiro

Ono kept on trying. He poured great effort into the parts of the group project he could develop on his own. He also made a friend who helped him with his English. Eventually, he impressed his professors enough to earn research funding to continue his studies.

Hiro on the campus of the Massachusetts Institute of Technology.

Inventor feature:
Crossing the ocean to reach the stars cont.

" I realized later that what filled me up in my first days at MIT was not a real confidence. Rather, I simply expected to be successful there because I had been successful back home. My confidence was like the air in a balloon, which goes away quickly once the balloon is punctured. Real confidence is strong and enduring, like a brick wall. You build up accomplishments, trust, and friendships as if piling up bricks, one by one. " —Hiro

Ono eventually landed his dream job at NASA's Jet Propulsion Laboratory (JPL). This is the same place where the **probe** Voyager 2, which inspired Ono as a child, had been built.

" Science and technology offer the promise of a career in which you can be judged for who you are, not where you are from. At JPL, no one cares what ethnicity you are or what race or what religion. We have engineers from all over the globe. **"** —Hiro

Ono has written a memoir in Japanese detailing his successes and struggles. The title roughly translates to *Crossing the Ocean to Reach the Stars*.

Hiro poses with a replica of the Mars rover Curiosity.

An expensive harpoon

The **tether** is not the only part of an **asteroid**-hitching craft that will have to be made of tough stuff. The harpoon must also be built to withstand the high-speed impact.

" We have conducted *simulations* [experimental tests] that show that it is really dependent on the incoming speed. If the relative velocity is 0.9 miles [1.5 kilometers] per second, there is no problem. You can use a regular metal like tungsten to safely attach to the asteroid. **"** —Hiro

The harpoon hits the target with the same relative velocity as the space **probe** is traveling. For Ono's asteroid-hitcher, the target speed is 6 miles (10 kilometers) per second.

" That is faster than the speed of a missile shot out of any cannon that we have. If you create the harpoon out of regular metal, it will be *disintegrated* [destroyed] instantly. **"** —Hiro

To hitch an asteroid at the target speed, the harpoon will have to be made of the hardest material known—diamond.

" At that speed, even with diamond, the collision will disintegrate about 30 percent of the harpoon material. **"** —Hiro

Diamond (right) is the hardest material known. Because of its hardness, it is used in many industrial cutting and grinding jobs. (below).

Playing out the line

❚❚ You are pulled by the rope, and you hold tight. If the rope does not break, then you can stop. **❚❚** —Hiro

Harpooning an **asteroid** is one thing. But even with the strongest **tether** imaginable, Ono's craft cannot just jerk to a stop. The sudden jolt would snap the tether or destroy the craft. Instead, the asteroid-hitching craft will have to release additional tether.

Think of an *angler* (person who fishes) who has just hooked a big fish. As soon as the fish is hooked, it starts to swim away. The angler does not just jerk on the line. If she did, the line might snap, and the fish would get away. Instead, she lets out more of her line, enabling the fish to flee. But as the fish flees, she applies tension to, or pulls back little by little on, the line. This tension eventually slows the fish down, enabling the angler to reel it in.

In a similar way, Ono's **probe** would slowly reel out additional tether. As it did, the probe would also apply a braking force, gently reducing the relative velocity to zero. Then the probe and asteroid would be moving along at the same speed, allowing the probe to eventually land directly on the asteroid.

Braking

The **asteroid**-hitcher will be able to release 60 to 600 miles (100 to 1000 kilometers) of **tether.** But even with that length, it will take tremendous braking force to slow the relative velocity to zero.

An object in motion has a kind of energy called kinetic energy. According to the principles of physics, energy cannot be created or destroyed. It can only be converted from one form into another.

Remember our express train on Earth? The train can stop by applying its brakes. This causes the brake pads to rub against the wheels, creating friction. Friction converts much of the train's kinetic energy—the energy of its movement—into heat. As the train slows, this heat can be transferred to the air or taken away by a cooling system.

At a relative velocity of 6 miles (10 kilometers) per second, our asteroid-hitcher has tons of kinetic energy. The craft can slow itself by applying a brake to the tether as it plays out, but such braking would produce tremendous heat.

❞ Heating is a big challenge. We have to come up with materials that can withstand a much higher temperature. We also need a more efficient way to *dissipate* [remove] the heat. **❞** —Hiro

But wait—all spacecraft need energy. Perhaps, thought Ono, we should put all that energy to use, instead of getting rid of it.

Big idea:
Regenerative braking

❝ When you apply a brake, you usually turn kinetic energy into heat and then dump it. Why not use that energy instead? ❞ —Hiro

It is not an entirely futuristic idea. In fact, this strategy is already widely used in hybrid automobiles. A hybrid automobile runs on a combination of gasoline and battery power. The goal of a hybrid automobile is to use energy more efficiently. One of the ways hybrids achieve this goal is through a process called regenerative braking.

Instead of applying a brake pad to the spinning wheel, the wheel is connected to an electric generator. The wheel spins the generator, producing electric power. The car slows as the kinetic energy is converted to electricity. The power generated is used to recharge the car's battery.

❝ So the car generates electric energy when it stops, and then uses that energy to get going again. **❞** —Hiro

Likewise, the **asteroid** hitcher could use the kinetic energy of the line as it is released to power a generator. Converting this energy to electricity would in turn slow the craft.

❝ It would also help to *mitigate* [reduce] the heat. **❞** —Hiro

The electricity generated could be used to power the **probe's** scientific instruments. It could also be used to gradually reel the tether in, bringing the probe to a soft landing on the asteroid.

Some hybrid automobiles use a process called regenerative braking to recharge their batteries. Hiro's hitcher would generate power in a similar way.

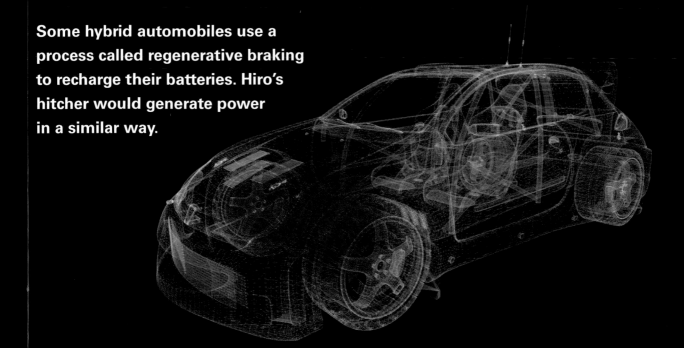

the sun

The ability to generate electric power through regenerative braking opens up a new range of exploration for the **asteroid** hitcher—the outer **solar system.**

❚❚ Spacecraft in the inner solar system, for example in the Main Belt, can generate electric power using *solar cells* [devices that use sunlight to produce electricity]. In the outer solar system, such as the **Kuiper belt**, you are too far from the sun to produce much solar power. **❚❚** —Hiro

In the past, outer solar system craft sometimes relied on nuclear power, generated through the *decay* (breakdown) of radioactive materials. But nuclear power systems are heavy and expensive, unlike the regenerative brakes.

There are two other factors that make the asteroid hitcher a good candidate for exploring the outer solar system. First, most **Kuiper belt objects** are too small to have a strong **gravitational pull,** making traditional **orbit** difficult. Second, spacecraft must travel extremely rapidly to get there in a reasonable time. The New Horizons **probe,** launched in 2006, is one of the fastest ever built. It took nearly 10 years to reach Pluto. When it got there, it sped by at a blistering relative velocity of 6 miles (10 kilometers) per second.

New Horizons captured this photograph of Pluto as it flew by.

A local train in the outer solar system

Engineers are still working to develop the materials and other technologies that will make the **asteroid**-harpooning hitcher a reality.

But Ono can already envision what a future mission might look like.

Launched from Earth, the asteroid hitcher would take about 10 years to reach its first target KBO. Approaching at about 6 miles (10 kilometers) per second, the craft would deploy its harpoon.

In this illustration, a probe reels in its tether to land on an asteroid.

❚❚ It is really like a local train, which stops at every single station. You can explore multiple asteroids or **Kuiper belt objects** [KBO's] in a single mission. **❚❚** —Hiro

With the harpoon stuck into its target, the **probe** would begin to release the **tether.** As the tether releases, the craft would use regenerative braking to slow its relative velocity and to generate electric power. With the relative velocity reduced to zero, the craft can use some of the power to reel itself to a landing on the KBO.

There, the asteroid hitcher could use special cameras, robotic arms, and other scientific equipment to study its surroundings. When the probe has learned all it can, it becomes time for one final trick— taking off again.

Taking off again

❝ You can do the reverse process, taking off by *retracting* [pulling back] the harpoon. **❞** —Hiro

Have you ever played tug of war with a prankster who suddenly let go of the rope? While you were both tugging, the force of your pulls balanced each other. When the other person let go, there was a sudden imbalance of, or difference in, force. This imbalance may have sent you sprawling in the opposite direction.

In the same way, the **asteroid** hitcher might take off simply by pulling on the harpoon. When the harpoon jerks loose, the craft will be nudged in the opposite direction—up and away from its landing site. A nudge may not seem like much, but remember that the target has only a weak **gravitational pull.**

Free of its target, the asteroid-harpooning hitcher could set course for another KBO and another tethered landing. In this way, it could move itself from target to target, vastly expanding our understanding of the **solar system** and its origins

Inventor feature:
Icy Moon Cryovolcano Explorer

Inventors often work on more than one idea at a time. Ono, for example, has also received a NIAC grant for his *Icy Moon Cryovolcano Explorer*. A cryovolcano is like a volcano but made of ice. It erupts, or pushes out, water and ice instead of lava and rock. Ono is designing the explorer to visit a cryovolcano on one of the icy moons of the outer planets. The craft would land near the volcano and lower a **probe** into it.

An artist's impression of a cryovolcano.

Masahiro Ono and his team

From left to right: Marco Quadrelli, Chen-Wan Yen, Gregory Lantoine, Paul Backes, and Masahiro Ono

Glossary

asteroid (AS tuh royd) a rocky or metallic body smaller than a planet that orbits the sun.

fly-by when a spacecraft passes by a body in space without stopping.

gravitational pull (GRAV uh TAY shuh nuhl pul) an attraction that objects exert on one another as a result of their mass.

Kuiper belt (KY puhr behlt) a region of icy objects in the outer solar system, beginning around the orbit of the planet Neptune. The Kuiper belt is also called the Edgeworth-Kuiper belt or the trans-Neptunian disk. An Irish scientist named Kenneth E. Edgeworth suggested in 1943 that the belt existed. The Dutch-born American astronomer Gerard P. Kuiper described it in more detail in 1951.

Kuiper belt object (KBO) any of the icy objects found in the Kuiper belt.

mass the amount of matter—the stuff that everything is made of—in something.

molecule (MOL uh kyool) one of the basic units of matter. A molecule is the smallest piece into which a substance can be divided and still have the chemical identity of the original substance.

orbit (AWR biht) a looping path around an object in space.

planetesimal (PLAN uh TEHS uh muhl) any of the smaller bodies that collided and stuck together to form the planets and other large objects in the solar system.

probe (prohb) a robotic spacecraft.

solar system (SOH luhr SIHS tuhm) the sun and all the planets, moons, and other objects that revolve around it, including Earth.

tether (teh TH uhr) a long, strong cord used to connect two objects in space.

For further information

Want to learn more about diamonds?
Hubbard, Judith. *What Are Diamonds, and How Do They Form?*
In Depth Science. CreateSpace Independent Publishing, 2016.

Want to experience putting objects into orbit?
Download this app: *Orbit – Playing with Gravity*. HIGHKEY Games,
2016. (The ad-free version is available online for a small fee.)

**Want to learn more about the New Horizons exploration to
Pluto and the Kuiper belt?**
Carson, Mary Kay and Tom Uhlman. *Mission to Pluto: The First Visit
to an Ice Dwarf and the Kuiper Belt*. Scientists in the Field. HMH Books
for Young Readers, 2017.

Think like an inventor

Imagine a long, strong cord like the tether on the asteroid-harpooning
hitcher. What other uses can you think of for such a cord, both in
space and down here on Earth?

Acknowledgments

Cover	© Cornelius Dämmrich
5	NASA/JPL
6-7	Peter the Whaler, colour lithograph by James Edwin McConnell; Private Collection (© Look and Learn/Bridgeman Images)
8-9	NASA/JPL-Caltech/T. Pyle (SSC)
10-11	Johns Hopkins University Applied Physics Laboratory/Southwest Research Institute (JHUAPL/SwRI)
13	Hiro Ono
14-15	NASA
17	ESA/Rosetta/MPS for OSIRIS Team MPS/UPD/LAM/IAA/SSO/INTA/UPM/DASP/IDA
18-19	© Cornelius Dämmrich
21	NASA/JPL-Caltech
23	© Science Photo Library/SuperStock
25	© enot-poloskun/iStockphoto
27	Hiro Ono
29	Hiro Ono
31	© Matteo Chinellato, ChinellatoPhoto/Exactostock/SuperStock; © David Tadevosian, Shutterstock
32-33	© genesisgraphics/iStockphoto
34-35	© Ortodox/Shutterstock
37	© devrimerdogan/Shutterstock
38-39	NASA/Johns Hopkins University Applied Physics Laboratory/Southwest Research Institute
40-41	© Cornelius Dämmrich
42	© Stocksnapper/Shutterstock
43	© Walter Myers, Science Source
44	Hiro Ono